Start <u>Now</u> in Oil

Start Now in Oil

TOM ROBB

AURUM PRESS

First published 1994 by Aurum Press Limited
25 Bedford Avenue, London WC1B 3AT

A catalogue record for this book is available from the
British Library

ISBN 1 85410 282 6

10 9 8 7 6 5 4 3 2 1
1998 1997 1996 1995 1994

Printed in Belgium by Proost

Contents

INTRODUCTION

Painting is something that comes naturally to every child. Colour comes from pencils, sticks or crayons, or poster paint. It only takes a few minutes to make a house with a few straggly lines; the window takes time and effort, but then the proud artist hands you the finished picture, makes sure you pin it up on the wall, and runs off to play with the kitten.

It's only as we grow older and more self-conscious that painting becomes difficult. The more aware we become of how hard it seems to take what we see or what we imagine and put it on a blank canvas, the more hesitant we are about our own skills. And all too often a first trial is so far from what we want that discouragement and despair make sure we'll never try again.

That's an experience shared by far too many people, and this series is here to prove to you that it doesn't have to be like that. We've set out 30 exciting projects, each with an introductory page which lets you practice some of the techniques before you begin.

And then we hope you'll find within a very short time you'll be painting pictures you can hang up with pride. In other words, you learn by doing.

You can start now, without a long introduction to complicated equipment, techniques and exercises. Learn by making pictures, right from the very first page – pictures that are fun to paint and pictures you can pin up and display as you absorb lessons in skill and application by doing rather than reading.

Oil paints are miraculous tools. The rich colours and smooth textures that come flowing out of the tubes are ready for you to use. They're the most flexible medium, too; you can scrub away mistakes or just paint over them. You can mix new colours on the palette and they'll look just the same on the canvas.

And they work on so many different supports – you can ply your brush happily on canvas, wood, or even paper with oil sketching pads.

So no more doubts. Pick up a brush, turn the page and start!

Tom Robb
Phoebe Phillips (editor)

PART ONE: STARTING NOW!

Oil is often described as the most prestigious medium for professionals, but it's even more exciting for new artists.

You'll find it useful to have a permanent storage place to keep everything tidy. An old table is ideal – even better if it has drawers for storing rags and so on. I use quite a few brushes (see the Shopping Guide) but to start with just buy one small sable, Size 0; a medium round and a medium flat, Number 4 and Number 5; and one larger Number 10.

A smooth piece of board can be used as a palette, and you'll also need a few china cups, an old rag or two and a palette knife, as well as a box to hold the tubes and another for the mixers and cleansers (linseed oil, turpentine, white spirit, etc.). Look through the Shopping Guide for more detailed information.

Because oil is so adaptable, you can choose to work standing or sitting, whatever feels most comfortable to you, so an easel is useful but not essential. I often prop up my canvas on an open box of paints, particularly when I'm painting outdoors.

You can also choose a medium sized canvas or two, as well as some pads of oil sketching paper. They will be ideal for all the individual projects. As a bonus, they are reasonably inexpensive and very easy to carry around. Don't buy anything smaller than A4, or larger than A3.

We begin with simple projects which nonetheless explore some of the fundamental techniques you are going to need through-out your future as an artist. So, having assembled your tools, don't delay a minute longer.

Project 1

Celery

Find a whole celery which still has all its leaves. If you can't buy one (or grow one!), look for a picture in a seed catalogue. Start by mixing a fresh green colour, using plenty of yellow. Don't add any oil or turpentine; the paint should be reasonably thick, dry rather than runny. Take up a number 4 brush, and practise long, curving strokes. I hold my brush in the middle or even near the end to give the brush plenty of space to move up and down. Keep your grip as light as possible, enough to give you control but not so tight that the movement becomes jerky. Go on making strokes even when the paint is running out – that will give you the textured effect of dry brushing.

The leaves are simple splodges made by putting the brush down carefully and lifting it off again without any movement on the canvas. A wider brush will give you bigger leaves. Try putting the edge of the brush down first , placing it at the bottom of where you want the leaf; the hairs will splay sideways a little to give you a nice fan shape.

When you start the project on a fresh canvas, be bold and fill the whole area. Begin with the long outer sticks, remembering that they curve a little into the base. Then add the leaves – in reality they are usually different sizes, so keep the splodges spontaneous and light and well-varied in shape and texture. You'll find it exciting to do so much with just one colour.

Butterfly

There is nothing monochromatic about this; here's a vibrant, almost manic sweep of primary colours, the pattern based roughly on a book of tropical butterflies which I found in the library.

Abstraction can be dry, remote and intellectual, but here it's been used as a way of playing with the essence of a magnificent natural form, and turning it into a painterly image with its colour and rhythms intact. And what fun!

Start by looking for a photograph of an animal or insect or a flower. Look for a pattern that really attracts you for itself rather than as a picture of a subject. In this case I was also anxious to find something to make up with primary colours – we'll be using a lot of subtle mixes later on, but it's a good thing to restrict yourself now and then to the three primaries, red, yellow and blue.

The wing of this butterfly was a wonderful swirl of interlocking circles. Transferred to canvas, I can make them as broad or as tiny as I wish. I used a big beautiful Number 10 brush, and laid on the paint with vigour and enjoyment.

Start by isolating your chosen pattern and put down the main features in a sketch, playing around with the various elements, and seeing how they might work on a broad scale. I chose the interlocking circles because they lend themselves to big round swings of the arm to suit the size of the brush. There's a correlation between brush size, brush stroke and speed; in general, the bigger the stroke, the quicker you paint.

It's sometimes hard to get going with a big brush after you've been concentrating on putting each stroke down carefully. Don't let your arm and wrist tighten up, or you'll make short jerky stabs instead of long sweeps.

Leaving a narrow white band between the colours will make sure they sparkle, no matter how intense or overwhelming the finished pattern might be.

Even if you prefer to cover every inch of the canvas, start with separated colours, and then you can work into the centre of the white space from each side, painting carefully with a small brush until the white disappears. If you try and do this when you first paint the circles, the sweep and liveliness of your brush strokes will also disappear.

Project 3   Study

Artist's Studio

This is a first step towards discovering how much variety you can achieve with simplified shapes which are freely drawn, flowing in easy brush strokes and using basically the primary colours.

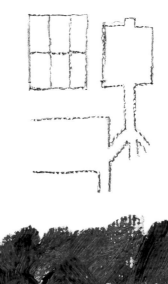

To start, I took a corner of my room and made a pencil drawing, translating the easel, table and window into simple rectangles. You can use any room and any furniture, but working with a studio easel gave me a strong shape and the opportunity to add lots of other colours.

Experiment with various brush strokes, using a good, strong background colour. You want to achieve lots of movement and texture in the paint, but with short strokes rather than sweeping movements. That way the surface seems lively but controlled.

To see the difference, try out a small section using a wide, even stroke, without lifting the brush from the canvas. See how calm and quiet that space becomes.

When I was happy with the surface texture, I worked all around the drawn figures with ultramarine blue, and then inside with white titanium for the window and the table top. If you prefer, you can create a contrast by making the white areas cool and smooth.

Now add the colour. The link between the colours on the palette and the colours on the painting is obvious – you may prefer to make them totally different, just to confuse the viewer! The one stroke of yellow on the easel lifts the whole picture into another dimension – try it without that and you'll see what I mean. Remember that when you want a colour to really sparkle, leave a little white around the edges.

There's also the subtle contrast between the colours on the palette, jumbled together as they would be when you paint, and the seemingly haphazard but really precise single brush strokes of colour on the painting. You might want to indicate a picture of some kind.

One of the obvious differences which you will find if you have worked in other mediums is that, while in watercolour or pastel you often leave the white paper to show through, with oil even the plain white areas need the added texture of paint on canvas to stand up to the strong, three-dimensional statement of blue, red and yellow.

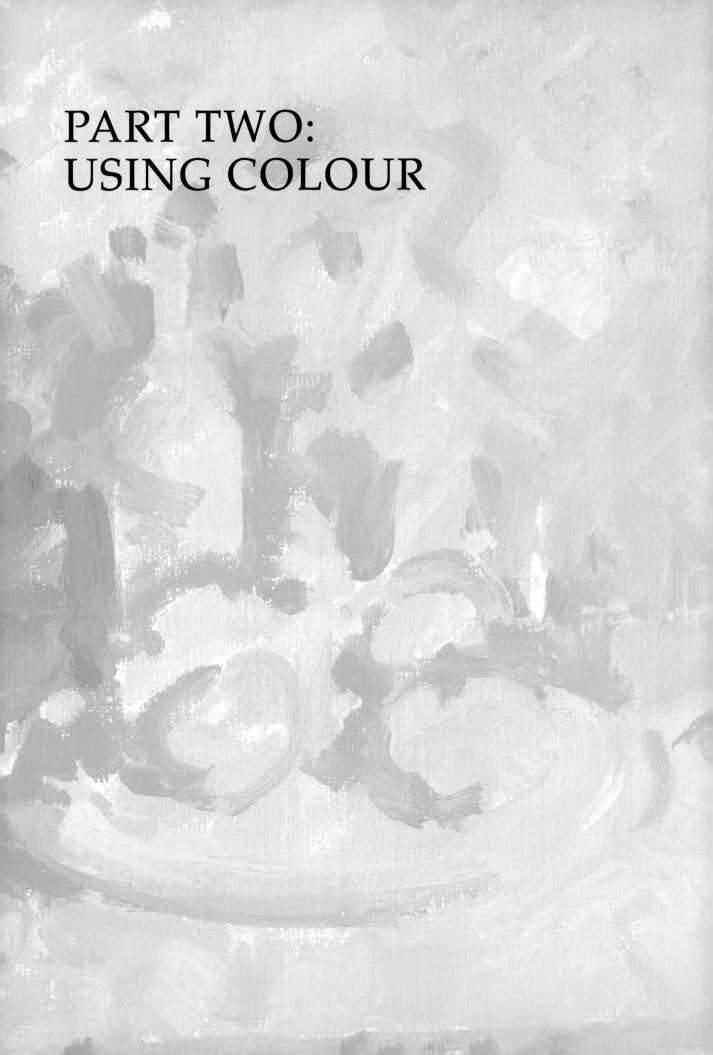

PART TWO: USING COLOUR

Of all the attributes of oil, colour and texture are the most immediately appealing. Colour in this medium is rich, sensuous, glistening. It comes out of the tube like something alive, twisting and turning as you lay it on the palette.

To help yourself understand the medium a little better, you can read about paint in the Shopping Guide.

When you decide what colours to use, learn to put them out onto the palette in a consistent way. Work in a circle around the edge, leaving the central section for mixing and blending. I usually put the cool colours on the left, the warmer colours on the right, with white and black at each end, but most painters have their own personal order.

By establishing a pattern this way, you will be able to work quite quickly; your brush will go automatically to the right area and pick up the colour you want for that particular brush stroke.

Strangely enough, for such a rich treasure trove of texture and depth of colour there is one disadvantage in the oil medium: mixing subtle colours can be quite difficult. The different pigments are blended with varying amounts of oils to make them flow, and so some colours will overwhelm the others when you try to create new blends. Mauves, purples and lilacs are particularly hard to mix up yourself, and it's well worth the minor expense of buying them by the tube, already mixed.

You can make a colour chart for yourself by taking a sheet of paper and painting a good, thick stroke of every colour you have in the box. Then try mixing them. Any mix of two colours will usually work well. Any mix of more than three colours together usually ends in brown!

Make a note of any mixes that you particularly like and keep a record of them in a notebook.

Blue Plates

Blue is a very special colour, the tone of sea and sky; it was also one of the earliest stains made from the indigo plant for textiles, even for tinting the human skin.

Cobalt blue made from the mineral can be traced back at least to the ancient Egyptians. It was used by the Chinese from the 13th century on for their renowned blue and white porcelain, and it's still in use today for modern interpretations of both Chinese and Dutch designs. So when you begin to experiment with this marvellous colour, you're really dabbling in history!

You'll need a few blue and white dishes for your first still life. Blue is such an important element in oil painting that it's worth the effort to find a few blue and white pieces. If necessary you can use the painting as a guide, but it's more interesting when you are working from real things.

To look at how rich a variety you can achieve with just this one pigment, start your studies with an area using a light touch of cobalt in titanium white, then work in sample patches of dark to light blue, beginning on the left with pure blue from the tube, then half white, then mostly white.

Once you have mastered the different tones, start making shapes. Make a four-petalled flower by putting the brush down gently, ferrule at the centre, and repeating this in a ring. A tiny stroke makes the stem. Try making other flower shapes just as simply.

In this project you're aiming to start controlling the brush with confidence, so fill a whole page if necessary until you can place your brush with just the right amount of paint, and lift it off again, leaving a clean shape.

Now try a three-dimensional shape. Paint a simple oval in a mid-blue. With two strokes of dark blue on one side and a few white strokes opposite, it becomes a cup. Heighten the effect with extra white underneath the darker shadow. This is the gleam of light coming from the left. Finally add more shadows to help the illusion. When you start the full still life, keep the shapes nice and chunky, with simplified decoration. You'll be practising fine detail later. Remember that with oils, unlike watercolour, you needn't wait for the background to dry.

Interior, Green and Grey

Here's a fascinating project which is much simpler than it might first appear. I've painted a sofa in a bay window, lit from above, and with the light coming through the shutters to create intriguing patterns against the sun.

The palette I used was quite simple, just two greys, a blue-grey, and two greens.

Using a limited palette allows you to explore how much you can achieve with very few colours, and also how much scope there is for contrast and subtle counterpoint of one against the other.

I put out the colours before I began, blending white and a touch of black to make grey. Yellow ochre and a touch of viridian gave me the softest of greens, with added white for the lighter shades. And in the shadows, an even lighter touch of ultramarine gave bluey depths for both grey and green.

The setting was easy to find – most of us have a sofa or chair underneath a window which would do just as well. The shutters here are particularly easy to paint, with their louvres making a strong regulated pattern in the window, but a set of curtains could replace them easily.

I was working in soft, late afternoon light which was quite white, but a bright sunny morning might mean adding lemon yellow to the white squares of the window. If you do that, remember that the reflections of light which show up white on the sofa here would also be more yellow, reflecting the sun through the glass.

Begin with the briefest of pencil touches to put in the proportions of window to sofa. In this case it was important that the windows were long enough to be the dominating feature, as they are in this room.

Perspective is very interesting here, too. The sofa was straight in front of me as I stood facing it. Behind it, the windows were set into an angled bay, as the top of the windows and the break in the ceiling makes clear. But because I was standing almost on a level with the tops of the lower shutters, they looked to me as if they went straight across behind the sofa instead of being angled – an example of painting what you see instead of what you imagine must be there. Had I been doing an exercise in perspective, I would have angled their tops to coincide with the tops of the windows.

Market Fruit Stall

Working with a full palette of bright colours is an exhilarating experience, and certainly nothing that most of us will see in an ordinary day's travel is as full of colour as a fruit stall. If you have a market near you, try and set up on the spot, although I admit it's not easy to find somewhere out of the way of busy shoppers. Otherwise, take a colour snapshot and work at home, or make a quick sketch using just a pencil to outline the shapes and write in the colours on the page.

Here one of the problems to solve is how to layer colours as well as making them bright, clean and crisp. Optics tell us that we see colour differently when the background is changed, so I've included

yellows and oranges on both blue and green. The rectangular shape of the market boxes give structure to an otherwise chaotic display. Start by painting in careful squares. Use a Number 6 brush, which will give you enough width but controllable edges. You can make them any colour you like – the important thing is that they are strong colours, with reasonably straight sides. Draw in the squares in pencil first if you aren't sure of your geometric abilities!

Cover the areas well, but without the textures of the previous studies. Make the coverage as smooth as you can to give added contrast to the rougher shapes of the fruit.

Now use a Number 4 brush to lay in the fruit. You needn't wait for the background to dry – that's one of the pleasures of oil paint – but you do have to be careful not to press down too hard or you will push through the layer you are putting down and start picking up the background colour.

Try an assortment of colours and sizes – see how the same red and yellow works against blue and then against green. Remember to vary the sizes, too; without wanting to draw in too many details, you do need to give a sense of how the market stall looks, and the sizes make different patterns for the eye, from tiny limes to huge cabbages.

When you begin your painting, start with the awning or some sort of feature across the top – it could be a store sign. This gives a little depth to the composition without being too realistic. The area between the top of the stall and the awning is filled

with restless shadows. I had originally painted in the lad serving customers, but it seemed to make it too precise, so I painted him out and left the slashed and jerky texture of the paint to make the same, busy effect.

Try it both ways for yourself. This is another of the assets of oil paint: you can experiment right on the canvas, changing your mind, moving things around, and keeping your options open until the paint begins to dry in a day or two.

If you want to get right back to the canvas, the best tool is a thin, flexible palette knife to scrape off as much paint as possible, and if needed you can finish off with a good scrub with turpentine or white spirit. But usually it's enough to scrape off the surface without scrubbing, because the paint you put on afterwards will cover up anything underneath.

PART THREE: TEXTURES

The texture of oil paint is compelling and totally tactile. No other medium of painting can be as three-dimensional and full of character, not only in its gradations of highs and lows but in marks it leaves of individual brush strokes.

An intelligent viewer can even tell something about the joyous confidence or troubled anguish of the artist when the painting was made by the way the brush strokes have been made and, even in their absence, an ultra-smooth finish will indicate hours of careful and painstaking work.

Texture also comes from the paint quality, of course. Oil paint thinned with turpentine can be as watery and faint as the lightest watercolour wash, while paint straight from the tube, and trowelled on with a palette knife, will be positively sculptural in its appearance.

Making the subject and its texture agree or contrast is one of the games we can play with oil pigments. Flat surfaces can be embellished with carefully detailed patterns for one effect, while the same surface with boldly scrolled designs will look very different.

The canvas has its part to play, too, when its grain can be used to the full or disguised by heavy underpainting.

In the three projects here, I've run the gamut from controlled swirls to create an impressionistic and emotional sky, through a patterned picture as flat as a Japanese print, to a rich floral grouping where each petal seems to grow out of the paint.

Clouds

Often it's enough to suggest a seascape or landscape with nothing more than a few hints; the viewer's imagination does the rest. Here's a project with big, sweeping movements that will help to free your arm and wrist from any constraining inhibitions.

This kind of brush stroke needs practice in getting rhythm into your hand so that the ripples and curves are big and generous and flowing. Think of it as conducting an orchestra, with a gentle curlicue in the air where the clouds roll.

When you are ready to start the painting, lay in a low-key background over the entire canvas, making sure the strokes go right across the area from edge to edge. Use enough paint to leave a nice thick texture on the canvas; I changed colours slightly by adding a little white to one stroke, a little black to another. This makes the painting much more interesting as imagination turns the modulations into sand or marshland.

The darkest brush stroke may be billowing waves or a distant shore. The curves above should give the impression of clouds on a stormy night. A touch of green from trees in the distance is reflected in the sky. Remember to keep the rhythm flowing right across the painting. Try an exercise by working on a much larger area, at least two feet across. You'll need that kind of sweep when you move on to wider landscapes.

Be bold and simple; the more detail I put into an atmospheric painting like this, the worse it gets.

Take up enough paint on a Number 6 or 7 brush, and circle across the whole sketchbook, going from side to side without raising the brush. Then do it over again with a blending colour to emphasize the swinging lines.

Once you have a free, easy movement, you can control it a little by keeping the line straight until the middle, giving a little squiggle and then trailing off. You musn't break off the stroke at any time, or it will lose the flow. Practise with different colours; try making a broad-brush background first in a lighter tone, to add richness to the result.

Umbrellas

A complete contrast in every way, this project is all about slow, careful painting with thinned-down colour.

I found a wonderful group of umbrellas stuck haphazardly into my hall stand. If yours are all black or brown, borrow your children's or some bright cheap patterned ones from a friend.

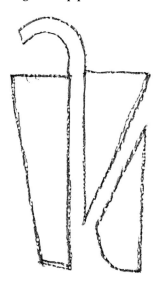

The design made by all the handles is really quite confusing. For your sketch, draw a few individual umbrellas and their handles first so you have a pattern to work on.

Using a narrow, flat brush, either a Number 2 or a 3, thin the paint with turpentine or linseed oil and work carefully over the pencil drawing, keeping the colour as thin and as flat as possible. At the same time, you need to try and keep your wrist loose or it will tighten up and your strokes will be jerky and out of control. It may be better to paint small areas and then relax for a few minutes before you try the rest. Oil paint lets you work at your own pace without leaving obvious joins.

The polka dots can be painted in two ways; either you leave white dots in the black, or you paint the black and then add white circles. You'll need a very small brush, perhaps a Number 0 or 1 sable round.

When you start the painting, make sure the image fills the page. Keep the painting as even as possible, without any shadows or modulations. Try to hold the brush well down the handle so you can work without your hand smudging the paint. Thin paint will dry relatively quickly, but this is still oil, not watercolour, so don't rush it too much. You may have to wait a few days to paint adjoining areas. I didn't leave white spaces between the colours this time; it would spoil the effect of the pattern of flat colours.

Vase of Roses

From a skim of colour to luscious thick scoops of pigment, oil is responsive to the painter's every wish. This project uses a palette knife instead of a brush. The techniques always remind me of cake decoration and as a great supporter of teatime luxury, I see nothing reprehensible in that!

A narrow flexible knife is the best to begin with, as you can control the paint more easily. Start by trying out the background. Pick up a relatively small amount on the top third of the spatula and lay it sideways onto the canvas. Continue the stroke down to cover a smallish area. The texture should be fairly smooth in the middle, with two heavier lines at the side. Lay three or four strokes like that side by side so they overlap. Each time the palette knife will leave a slightly different texture.

The roses are made very simply with three tones of pink to create modelling, and white for extra sparkle. Practise laying them against each other and lifting off sharply until you can keep the colours quite separate. Don't try to have six or seven intermediate colours until you can handle a knife as easily as a brush.

Work in masses rather than lines; you are not trying to create a subtle effect but rather an impressionistic one. The thick edges of the strokes will catch the light, giving additional shine and sparkle to the painting.

Now start making shapes with the knife, curving your strokes to create petals, and laying the paint down in short straight lines for the leaves and stems. Practise putting down and lifting the knife cleanly, so the rich ribbons of pigment stay where you want them to.

When you begin the project itself, lay on a flattish background, then the vase, and only then add the flowers. Finish by laying down a variety of strokes on the background to balance the texture of the vase and roses.

PART FOUR:
SPECIAL EFFECTS

When you begin to work in oil, you'll soon realize how easy it is to create all sorts of special effects which are technically much more difficult in other mediums.

This is partly because oil is fundamentally opaque and it can hide anything underneath, but also because it can be worked and blended right on the canvas or oiled paper, which means that you can see what is happening while you work, and change it according to whether you are pleased or dissatisfied with the result.

It is also simpler to work with because for much of the time the medium is meant to be seen from a reasonable distance, and this gives us much more leeway in leaving out detail.

We can sketch in windows and doors with the lightest of touches, yet the impression will be there.

Blending colours, too, can be as meticulous as in the work of the Old Masters or as simple as two threads of paint laid side by side and trowelled together with a knife like cake icing.

Reflections can be shown as a precise rendering of the original image painted upside down, or as impressionistic as a few flecks of white, which is all you would see of sails in a rough sea or a face in an old, darkened mirror.

Add these techniques to your repertoire, and then another dimension opens up of atmosphere and imagery. It's up to you to look out for surprises every day in the visual world all around.

Unusual references give yet another dimension; a subtle dawn sky behind a clump of houses instead of trees, or a reflected skyscraper in a rain puddle.

The Embankment

Blending is an essential tool for the artist, creating modulations and changes in tone as well as colour. In this painting it was used to take the eye smoothly from the darkness of the river walk to the deep blue of the evening sky.

Start by putting out a series of pigments on your palette – it's important that the bottom and top of the picture should have the same weight, and it's easier to see that if you make a small trial progression first. Use a reasonably large, flat brush – a Number 6 or 7.

Work in one direction – top to bottom or bottom to top, it doesn't matter, but if you try to work towards the middle from both ends you'll never get a smooth transition. I started from the dark brown, adding white for a lighter brown, then pink, a lighter pink, then blue.

Paint straight across the page, lifting your brush and starting again on the edge each time. Let the bands overlap, but make sure there's an area which is the pure colour you lay down.

The trees are simple short horizontal strokes of dark brown with a faint trail for the trunk. Keep the pigment fairly thick and the brush dry, so that the edges are indistinct and blurred, as the outlines would be in an evening light.

Putting it all together makes a misty night scene. I added a few dry-brush streaks of white to pick up reflected lamplight, which had just been turned on. Make it very, very light – you want a bit of a glow, not a glare. You might prefer a touch of ochre rather than white to keep the whole painting in a lower key.

A Bowl of Apples

The techniques involved in this still life are really quite simple. It relies on accurate observation of the colours and tones of the apple skins and the tones of the wooden bowl to make its effect.

Start by drawing a half circle so that you learn to work comfortably in a natural curve. This will prove invaluable for all sorts of subjects.

Lay down two tones of red, quite dry but not too thick. Add an inner curve of orange.

Now start blending the various reds by using a clean, dry brush and stroking over and over. Clean the brush off each time you finish one stroke, so that the brush blends rather than adds new colour. Leave an area of the original colour to act as an anchor – here it's the outer skin of dark red.

Most red apples have a little green or yellow in patches – work that in, too, but start with the smallest amounts of new colour – it's much easier to add more than to take away.

Look carefully at the fruit, and see what other colours it contains. I used pink rather than orange Lay the colours very close together, to give you a base before you start blending.

You'll also want to use colour to model the shape of the apple, giving you light and shadows. This means the tones of the colours should change, too, from dark, or heavy, to light. Look at the apples and decide where the shadows will come, and add a curve of your darkest colour there.

The little indentations around the stem and blossom end of fruit all help to model the shape, even without colour or any other detail. Use your paint to interrupt the smooth curves with a V shape, and at the base of the V draw up a stem. Use a very tiny Number 0 brush to add a little black edge for emphasis. Do the same at the blossom end.

Practise the same careful blending with a dry brush using the browns and greys of the bowl.

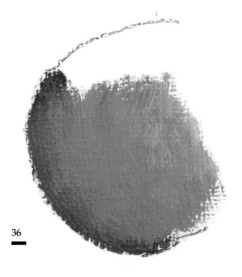

Moorings

One of the most enchanting techniques is creating reflections which can show two aspects of the same object. Reflections can be as clear as a mirrored image or as minimal as these boats, with only a ghostly touch of white in the water.

There's blending, too, of colour and texture; the blues of sea and sky use texture strongly for added contrast. The sky has been blended from three or four different light blues, and because the picture is painted from a fairly low viewpoint, it forms the background to the boats. The sea is a mass of thicker strokes in varied darker colours, but they are very near in tone so that they blend together in their own way.

Start by seeing how easy it is to paint boats with a few strokes. Give yourself a patch of plain blue, blending it carefully from three or four tones to add movement but still keeping the appearance of a clear sky. If you use only one colour it will always look artificially flat and boring.

Using a dry brush, Number 5 or 6, make some short horizontal strokes. Still with a dry brush, add details of cabin, mast, shrouds, and so on, keeping your hand so light that the paint misses now and then. A very precise line would look out of place unless the rest of the painting was just as detailed. Touches of yellow really light up the whole picture; all you need is the tiniest dot.

Reflections in water depend very much on the surface. Here choppy water allows only one strong reflection, the white hull which is trailed over the water. The masts are reflected as a zig-zag of white paint. Use a very dry brush so it only catches the canvas here and there.

On the left, above, you can see how widely spaced the reflections of the mast would be in a rough sea. On the right, smoother water gives reflections much closer together.

When you start the full painting, draw a line where you want the horizon, and then paint up and down for the two main areas of sky and water. All the details of the boats are added on top, including highlights of yellow and ochre.

Remember that the waves get larger as they get nearer the eye, so your strokes should be correspondingly wider – change to a Number 8 or 9 brush for the foreground and work vigorously, right across the canvas.

PART FIVE:
PAINTING LIGHT

Light shines on everything we see, because of course we wouldn't see at all without it! This makes painting light seem like one of the most difficult techniques to learn, because what we see is so transient.

And yet, those attributes make it possible for artists to paint light in a hundred different ways, for what you see will never be exactly the same as what I see. And what we see one day will be very different from what we see on a different occasion.

Every painting will be different, but we must all try to evaluate what we see, and transform it into paint as clearly as possible.

Outdoors it's all too easy to be overwhelmed by the great view in front of your easel. How can you begin with all the varying tints of green, the thousand sparkling edges of sunlight?…

The only way to make sense of it is to break down the picture from the whole scene to a very tiny part of the whole which you can concentrate on. Look at the nearby wall where the light colours one side pale yellow. Look at one of the mountains where the setting sun creates a golden edge to the green mass.

Work as quickly as you can because the light will change minute by minute. If you find that difficult, and you want more time to absorb what you are looking at, then freeze the moment by photography or, even better, by planning to come back to the same spot at the same time for a few days in a row.

There will be changes, like the changes in the weather, but they'll be natural changes which you can incorporate into your painting.

Inside the Barn

This is a very different aspect of handling colour – the changes that occur when the sun sends strong bands of bright light onto a subject.

I've painted from the interior of a shed looking out, to show the tremendous contrast. You could do the same study from inside a room or even a garden shed. Just make sure there is a substantial opening through which you can see the change from sunlight to shadow. A door is best, because there's the sharp difference of colour on the wood as well as on the ground. The sunlit band of colour will usually be a lighter tone, but sometimes, as with the door in the painting, the light is so strong that it creates the appearance of two colours.

Start your practice sheet by making up a series of coloured doors which are all opening on to a sunny yard. You should find that with that one change of colour you've achieved the appearance of sunlight coming through the opening.

Try out a small area of walling. In Project 3, you saw how short brush strokes could achieve a lively texture. Here I needed to explore the softer, more subtle texture of old plaster. The surface is painted first, then the darker markings are laid on by putting the brush down and lifting it off again in a random pattern. Look at walls in your home and try to reproduce their varying textures.

Perspective is the art of making things look as if they have real depth. The Old Dutch Masters knew that tiled floors were an easy way to show perspective, and most of their interiors have black and white tiled floors which add enormously to the effect.

Here the big stone paving slabs serve the same purpose. You don't have to draw in every one, or every dividing line, either. Practise sketching in just enough to make the right effect without the result looking like an exercise in floor-laying!

When you start your picture in earnest, see how the light outside also makes the outdoor colours much paler than usual. Heighten the bleached effect a little to give your painting extra contrast. Aerial perspective is covered more fully in Project 26.

Silver and Gold

One rainy morning I saw two glass bowls set out on the table, ready to be wrapped up as presents. One had a gold rim, the other silver.

The effect was tremendous in the grey light. The bowls themselves were as insubstantial as ghosts, only two flashes on their metallic rims catching the light – the perfect subject for a project on highlights.

Practise with a soft grey (or any soft quiet tone) as a background, the better to show off your prizes. Play around with the paint, smoothing it flat in some areas, adding slightly lighter and darker brush strokes in other places. The three tones of grey in the final picture are made with pure grey pigment at the top, a good third of flake white in the centre, and a touch of blue in the bottom half where the tablecloth disappears in hidden folds.

Try modelling simple shapes with lighter colour, creating areas of light and shadow that are far more subtle than a hard-edged design.

Loosen up your wrist so you can paint the oval tops in one confident motion. You can start with a drawn shape if you are hesitant, but make sure that when you start painting, you let the brush take you along instead of creeping step by step, following the pencil line.

When I looked at the highlights, light coming from the front glittered on one small spot. That's where you add a dash of brilliant yellow to the yellow ochre, a flick of pure white to the grey.

But don't miss where the highlights reflect a tiny speck of light on the opposite side of the circle. Those two additional sparks give all the dimension and presence the bowls need. Try it without the reflected highlights, and you'll see.

The vase of flowers was an addition to help the picture achieve depth and place – it seems to anchor the cloth, making what could look like a grey band into a tabletop. The touch of a few muted pink patches points up the only deep colour, the yellow ochre of the gold rim.

But looking at it later, I'm not sure whether I liked it better without the vase. When you can pin up your paintings on the wall, look at them critically even after you think they are finished. A few days later, you might recognize that it needs something added or taken away. In the latest version, I did take away the vase and flowers – but I still think it needs something, so I'll keep working.

Oil is a forgiving medium that way; it creates the problem of never knowing when to stop! Many of us go on tinkering with our paintings for years – the saying goes that a new painter never knows how to start, and an old painter never knows when to stop!

Harbour Evening

Light is such an important element in figurative painting that I would put it at the top of the list in terms of how it affects the viewer.

Think of the dark, side-lit portraits of Rembrandt, the great explosions of colour in Turner, the sun and shadow of the Impressionists. Handling the effect of light can teach you more about the art of painting than almost any other single subject.

In this third study especially concerned with light, looking into the evening sun turned the surface of the river to molten silver. So the whole picture becomes grey instead of the blue of our previous harbour scene (Project 12, The Moorings).

The difference between the two is more than just colour. In The Moorings, the sun was coming from behind me, and so the white boat on a blue sea was pretty straightforward. Here the boats against the light are dark shapes in front of the darkening horizon. The hulls have disappeared entirely, and except for the thin line of their masts, only a little light catching the tops of their bundled sails shows where they are.

If you can find a nearby harbour, check the setting sun times so that you can arrive at just the right time. Usually the water will be quiet, so lay the cool grey on flat, with only a few dark lines to show the tide is moving. Up in the sky the sun has been diffused by the clouds and the coming dusk. Vaguely pink, it scattered its light on the water as I scattered white on grey. Let a few more white lines drift across in the same direction as the dark ripples, and add a very light touch of pink for the reflected sunset. Nothing more is needed.

PART SIX: FIGURES

Figures in a landscape appear from the earliest paintings; they are sometimes an intrinsic part of the picture but they were also deliberately added even when the artist was looking at an empty view, in order to provide a sense of scale and proportion.

Sometimes, of course, the figure or figures are the most prominent part of the painting, and they should be treated more as a portrait – see Project 30 for some hints on how to make that work for you.

However, most outdoor scenes will benefit from having casual figures strolling about, chatting to each other in groups, or working at some task.

If you are outdoors, look for a café or a convenient wall where you can sit down, preferably slightly to one side of the main walkways, so that you gradually become part of the scene.

Start with a pad of oil sketching paper, just one or two tubes of paint, and a medium brush. drawing in the figures in simple strokes as quickly as you can.

Judge their size by the doorways or cars that you can see. Try to work unobtrusively – people become very self-conscious when they think they are being studied, and their movements become jerky and rigid, making it harder for the artist to capture the casual feeling which is exactly what you want!

Don't look for accuracy this time, just keep working for at least an hour. At the end you'll have a fluency in your wrist and figures that will surprise you!

Look carefully at what people carry or the tools they are using – a bag of shopping will weight someone down on one side. Remember that tiny detail will suddenly make a simple stroke into a person.

On the Beach

All through this book I've put down a lot of ideas which I have found useful in teaching, persuading you to try to use every part of the canvas, not to divide the painting in the middle, to keep the background and the figures in proportion, and so on.

But here is one, just for fun, which is the direct opposite of a lot of things I've been saying, and yet on its own terms it does work. Flat, simple shapes in silhouette have a particular charm recognized long before the 1930s posters for seaside towns.

Follow the instructions for sketching in tiny figures on Page 49, but keep them all dark brown. Most silhouettes are black, of course, but that would be too emphatic a colour against the sea.

Start by laying really flat areas with a medium brush, Number 5 or 6, where you want the sky, sand and sea. The geometry is emphasized by the division of ground and air into two equal parts, and the slightly angled chunk of sea. The straight brush strokes and smooth surface of the paint allow no texture to interfere with the strong triple division.

Try painting the umbrellas with as smooth an outline as possible – that's the key to all silhouette painting. The stem starts just below the top, leaving a dark space because of the shadow cast by the umbrella top. It's little touches like this that make the scene surprisingly realistic in spite of its stylized appearance.

Where the sea met the sand I left a line of white for the surf foam. Make sure all three colours are very flat, and let them dry; the figures must cover their background absolutely cleanly, and you can only be sure of that when the background is dry.

The result, when you've added a few lines of a towel or two, a single figure nearer the foreground and a beach basket in bright yellow, breaks every suggestion about modulating the foreground, adding movement to the sky, but I smiled all the time I was working on it! Especially the half-man in the water. Who said art is too serious to be left to artists? Not me.

Market Place, Italy

Being able to populate your paintings is quite an asset. While big landscapes can look magnificent without a sign of human presence, many need the sense of scale and proportion that human beings provide. City and town pictures would be frighteningly empty without someone, somewhere, and street scenes in particular are a lively and exciting way to paint when you travel.

Using a medium to large brush, draw some short strokes of different colours, almost but not quite touching.

Take a neutral colour, either grey, brown or ochre, and a smaller brush, very dry. Add the heads with just a small blob, a few trails for the feet, and a few lines running to one side for shadows. Giving an impression of a figure is often easier from the back or from the side than trying to paint in a face.

Practise creating windows on a few blank areas by drawing in parallel lines for facing windows, and receding lines of tiny strokes for buildings that are going away from you up the hill. Keep all the details as broad as you can; look at some of the Impressionist street scenes, and you'll see how little they use to create enormous and crowded avenues with minimal brush strokes.

Finally, add some extra colour and shape for dresses, a hat, a handbag. Little white spaces between the figure-strokes help to separate them and add air and space to the picture.

When you work on the main picture, start by dividing up the space into sky and town. Paint in the buildings very lightly, with just lines for roofs; by using a whole palette-ful of colour you can give the impression of a jumble of buildings from just a few painted spaces, with rows of dark strokes for windows. Add the figures at the end; they will bring colour and life to the scene, as they do in reality.

Cliff Scene

This was a particularly enjoyable project to paint. I love walking on the beach, and I'd been trying to find a subject which would point up the different way we see the same object in front of the light or behind the light.

The usual school example of optical changes is a circle of yellow inside a black square and then inside a white square, when the yellow-in-white seems larger than the yellow-in-black.

But here in front of me was an exciting image of colour and sizing changes which depended on the surroundings rather than an exercise, and was much more fun to paint.

Paint two bands of colour, one very dark, one very light. Draw a light figure on the dark band, moving the brush vertically – a smudge for the body, a dot for the head, a little trail for the feet. and arms. You'll need to use the Number 1 or 2.

Do the same with dark figures on the light band.

When you've finished three or four figures on each band, tack the page up somewhere, move back and look. The light figures on the dark background will look nearer to you and larger than the dark figures on the light ground. The effect is heightened because in all landscapes the foreground is always a darker tone than the paler, distant horizon.

You can see that very simply by playing around with bands of colours going from dark to light – it immediately starts to look like a landscape. If you reversed it and went from light to dark it would look like a skyscape.

When you start the painting, remember to keep the bands in the foreground wider as well as darker. You can use many more colours than just beachy-sand or rock grey. There are usually streaks of blue and yellow somewhere in the rock and an artist is allowed a little license to make them more obvious!

The light coming from behind the cliffs throws its effect onto the beach as well, so that there are streaks of bright yellow on the sand as well as on the edge of the cliff itself.

PART SEVEN:
MORE TECHNIQUES

Once you've begun to explore new horizons, technique and craftsmanship come to help you on the way.

Now you can start to develop individual skills, depending on the subjects and styles which you have made your own.

We've talked a lot about learning to see, but there are many fascinating aspects to this vital tool. Sometimes, as in Project 19, it's what you *can't* see that's important. There are bound to be times when you don't want to paint exactly what's in front of you, but perhaps a version which you would like to see, if only it were there! Then perhaps you can look at what's in the shadows instead of what is clearly in the light.

Another tool is the close-up view – seeing so clearly and in such detail that the entire object becomes a background, and the detail becomes your subject.

Glazes are another way of adding more variation to your paintings, by giving you a transparent effect seldom seen in oil. If you have worked in watercolour you know how effective thin glazes and washes can be. Oil can be handled in a similar way, although the paint will not run as quickly as water.

Of course you can combine all or any of these skills with others you have already practised, to create unusual images and special effects that work best for individual paintings. Always be willing to try out a new approach – you'll surprise yourself!

Flower Study

A great deal of painting is about learning to recognize what isn't there, and painting only what you actually see rather than what you think you see. We look at an object and our imaginations fill in all sorts of details, patterns, even complete shapes. All we need are a few suggestions, a line or two, a splodge of colour, and our minds do the rest.

Of course this is not just true of art, it's true of life. The ability of the brain to pick up tiny clues and provide rational assumptions is one of the things which separate us from computers. .

The philosophical approach which allows the artist to take down a painting to the merest suggestion is called minimalism, but this project is only a half-way house, because I'd like you to learn something about what can't be left out – just as important!

Start with a careful, traditional drawing. In this case I chose a single flower from a large pot. Try to encompass everything you think would be needed both for identification and to make a complete image. Make sure you put in the shadows where the colour grows darker.

Now start to paint. Use a coloured background even for your sketch because you want to make a note of where you have left out whole areas of the flower, and you may not see that so easily when the background is white.

Help your concentration by turning the light down extremely low, or half closing your eyes. A lot of the image will disappear and you'll see only a few twists of colour and perhaps a gleam from one brilliant touch of yellow on the stamens, The dark green leaves and stems will disappear completely.

Paint only what is actually in front of you; that will usually be enough. Resist the temptation to fill in the gaps – you would be beginning to paint what you know is there, not what you see.

The result, close up, will look like nothing but a few twisted lines and patches of colour. But step back and the spray of flowers is instantly completed by the mind. Make a few sketches and try painting out different areas to see what really has to be there. Use the drawing constantly to compare with your painting, and remind yourself of the original subject.

Fisherman's Box

For a complete change of focus, here is a project about the tiniest details you are likely to paint in oil – a set of fishing flies, every feather and striped wire caught in the prism of your observation.

You'll need the tiniest of brushes – Number 0 round sable. Work with the driest pigment, without a trace of extra oil or turpentine or the shapes will run away with you.

Practise making strokes which spring from a central point – these will be the feathers and wisps of material tied down to the fly. Try stroking lightly to leave only the faintest hint of a colour, or stroking more carefully, with a little added turpentine, to create the shape of the hook. Remember painting is about the texture of the object as well as the texture of the paint.

Now look at how delicately the box is made. Each mitred corner of mahogany changes colour slightly as the wood is turned. The shadows inside the cabinet are soft grey – the glass is indicated only by a few streaks of reflected light over the surface. Make sure they are all straight and run parallel to each other.

When you come to paint the picture, take as long as you like over each fly. You will need to control the brush very carefully. Inside the box, I painted the velvet lining first, and then – one of the few times I would stress this – you really need to let the paint dry, even if it takes four or five days. Although thicker paint can be worked right into a wet background without running, these delicate strokes could be damaged by something as small as a hair dragging in wet pigment.

Don't worry if your first trials look messy. This is not an easy project, and it takes patience and time to get it right. If you find it difficult to concentrate, do just one fly at a time. It will be worth it.

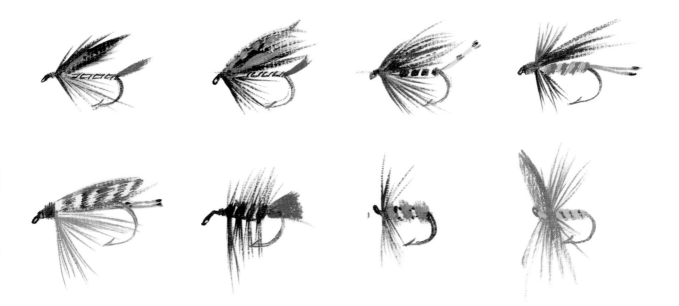
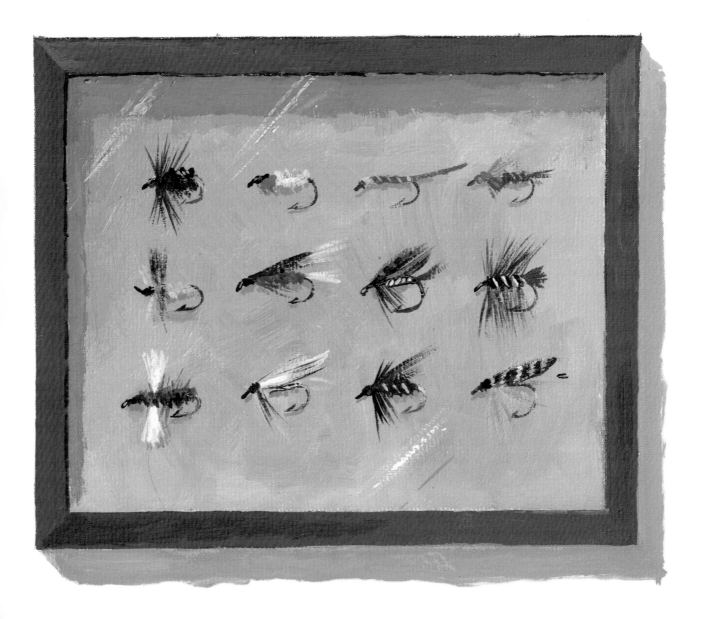

Provençal Village

Glazing in oil is not unlike glazing in watercolour, except that you will be using turpentine or turpentine substitute for the dilution instead of water.

Windows are an important part of landscape. They need never be laboriously painted in, pane by pane, but simply indicated on the building with short even strokes. The important image is one of regularity and grouping. Look carefully at the building to see how the windows fit into the façade – in twos, in threes, in singles? Look for the shadows of the time of day to give them depth, and remember they should correspond with the shadows on the building itself.

Stand well back from your simple strokes and you'll see how quickly they become a series of windows. Look at the paintings of traditional street scenes by famous artists – until you go right up to the canvas, you'll have believed that they carefully painted in each frame and each pane!

Start your landscape, using a very light brush in pale green to outline the shapes on the canvas. Put in the top of the hill, the big bulky building halfway down, the rock fall which interrupts the buildings, and the street at the bottom.

I'm going to let the primed canvas do the work of white, as I would with a watercolour. So all I need is to test the orange which will be the major colour of roof and rock. I want three strengths: light for the rock itself, darker for the underpainting of the roof, and heaviest of all for the accents on the tiles.

I used yellow ochre and a touch of red to mix orange on the palette. Then I put some on a scrap of canvas to see how thick it was. You'll see that the colours aren't really blended; that's deliberate, to get the effect of washed stone and rippled tile.

Then I added a little turpentine, and the paint became workable and much more like an average texture used for coverage.

A little more, and the colour was still too dark, the texture too thick. But then just one or two drops, and it began to run, just as I wanted it to.

I started to work with the viridian green and the ultramarine blue, washing them with the liquid paint but not tilting the canvas – I wanted them to stay where they were.

Working around the shapes of the buildings, I painted in the windows while the first wash was drying. It does take longer than watercolour - you'll have to wait hours or even overnight between layers. Finally I added a bit of the dark orange, and let it trickle down the roof, adding thicker strokes here and there for contrast.

PART EIGHT:
LOOKING BACK

Oil painting has such a rich history that the new artist can be totally bewildered when looking at the work of great masters of the past.

In fact, the problems that many of them faced are very similar to the problems of the rawest recruit. Van Gogh worried about his lack of training in drawing, Matisse knew he was sometimes called a decorator with colour instead of an artist, and Renoir struggled constantly to make the skin tones which he loved more and more luscious.

So these incredible masterpieces can help all of us, no matter how new to art, especially when we can pick out the particular problems which we have and look for their solutions – or at least their attempts to solve them!

But first we must look at how they approached their subjects and what they wanted to achieve in their paintings. For this, it is very useful as well as great fun to try our hands at their individual styles.

During the middle of the 19th century, the greatest revolution in painting since the Renaissance struck like a thunderbolt in Paris. The Impressionists had arrived. With them came a whole new approach to looking at objects, seeing shadows in colour instead of black, working with all the fervour of neophytes in the open air, far from the stale constraints of the studio.

Art would never be the same again. Today we can explore their work to see what it can teach us.

Château d'Albi

Oil painting has a rich history of changing techniques and fashions over the past four hundred years. No experiments were greeted with more disdain than the optical theories of the 1880s, when the work of Seurat and Signac created a style called Pointillism, their paintings constructed from small dots of colour.

Their contemporary critics were outraged just as much as today's viewers are charmed by 19th-century examples. Even though the theories have been discarded, the technique makes a fascinating project for any artist; some modern painters have revived pointillism and have made it serve their own, very successful styles.

Using one base colour, I build up a pattern with small dots of paint, keeping the paint fairly thin and flat. I use a second tone in the same way to create shadows and modelling. I sometimes leave white spaces to add light, but it can make the image look rather disjointed if there are too many gaps. I have to keep stepping back before continuing to paint.

Adding the other colours works in the same way – instead of brush strokes the images are built up with small patches (they are really dashes, not points, in spite of the name.)

Look closely at any Pointillist painting and you'll be able to see the separate strokes easily. Pointillist works are best seen from a distance – too near, and they dissolve back into dashes.

Mountain Landscape

A small, informal group of painters showed together in Paris in 1905. They believed that you could transform painting with strong colours emphasized and strengthened to become the dominating force in a composition. Matisse, Derain, and Marquet were among them, and their use of unnatural and vivid colourings – red sky, purple earth, and so on – earned them the nickname of Fauves, or Wild Beasts.

Within a few years most of the artists had turned to newer preoccupations, and the group, such as it was, had dissolved. But today their work is being re-assessed for its remarkable vitality and robust composition. Now, perhaps because we are sufficiently removed in time , we can appreciate their influence. Without a doubt they have changed our ideas about what we see and how to portray the landscape

One very sunny day the air was so bright with glittering light that the view was transformed. and within a few hours I had completed this sketch.

Above are the traditional colours which usually tell us we are looking at earth and sky. On the right are patches of the colours – purple and turquoise – that I could see in the autumn air. I put them down on the palette, just as you see here, and they instantly made their own landscape.

Paint a bold sketch like this quickly without giving yourself too much time to worry. Start with an overall background – you could be even more daring than I was and plump for good, fauve red! Then brush in the major elements – the misty hills, the trees, the furrowed earth in the foreground, and finally, still working as fast as you can, lay in small blocks of colour for the small elements like the houses and buildings. I didn't make any attempt to put in detail or precise forms.

Finally, I made sure that the brushwork had the same vitality and enthusiasm which I felt at the time. Instead of a serene arc of blue the sky was full of white and reflected yellows, the earth shimmering with red houses and blue roofs.

When you take a new approach to something as traditional as landscape, it's important to have the courage of your convictions and really let yourself go. A traditional brown and green field won't look much like a Fauve painting if you just add a few strokes of orange.

Begin by trying to see if there are some of the group's paintings in your local museum – at worst, there are illustrated catalogues and books which are full of magical achievements by all the leading members of the group. Who knows, you may become known as the Wild Beast of Bigelow Gardens.

The Chair

This project is definitely not about the object of its title. Inspired by Matisse's work, it's a painting of the senses. Red against orange, pattern against pattern, in a cacophony of design which makes you either shriek with agony or jump for joy. There's no middle ground here!

The Japanese prints so popular in Paris fascinated many of the leading artists at the turn of the century. They added their flat swirls of pattern to a much earlier European tradition of medieval illuminators, who patterned every surface with designs meant to emphasize the richness of their patrons and their ability to embellish and ornament all of life.

Both of these were highly stylized images, and both reinforced painters in their desire to shake up the politesse of academic art and move on from the natural and realistic studies of the Impressionists.

Pattern on pattern is not as easy as it looks – you need a unifying colour or motif which will let them blend and float together. Fashion today has gone back to Matisse's approach, so you can find plenty of subjects to inspire you in magazines.

The images you portray can be wild or controlled. Experiment with different ways to paint the same wallpaper – with broad brush vitality, or quieter, but just as effective, detail.

Keep the motifs balanced in size over all the surface, or you'll have problems with the central figure being distorted even more than you would wish! Remember that if you choose to paint fairly

flat and in detail you'll need a smaller brush, and a smooth background layer. Although you can work directly into wet paint, this method will benefit from at least one or two nights to dry before you add the pattern.

Once you are happy with the way you can put down the different colours then start your sketch by putting the chair or any small piece of furniture or even a patient sitter in front of your design.

Keep its outline as simple as possible, in order to let the patterns have centre stage without any competition. Nonetheless, it does give a sense of coherence to the painting and makes an effect markedly different from the all-over pattern of Project 25.

By sitting firmly on the floor it will also remind you that the carpet design is seen at an angle.

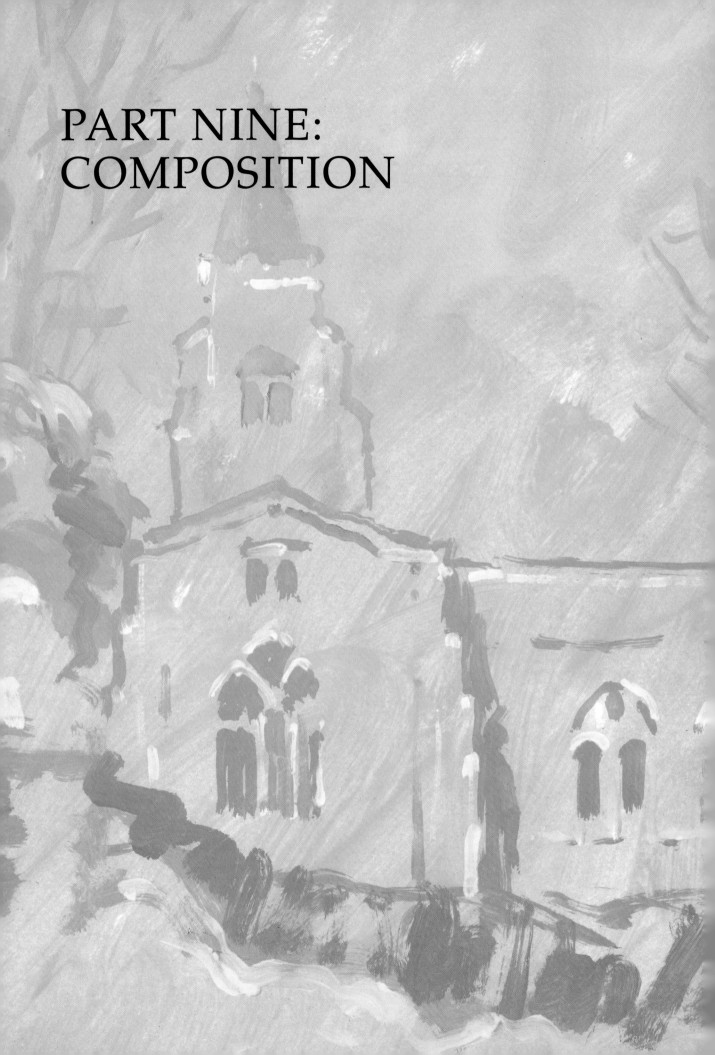

PART NINE:
COMPOSITION

It's time to take a look at the most important part of image-making: composition.

There are elements of composition common to all painting, but some special factors need to be considered when you are working in oil.

First, the very intensity of the colour, so deep and rich, can make it difficult to appreciate perspective and pattern – things that would be obvious in a drawing or a watercolour.

That's one reason why many artists begin with tone drawings and pencil sketches before they begin a major oil painting.

However, I do think that aside from a few marks to help you position your image on the surface, try to work out the composition directly onto the surface with oil, even if it's only a sketch. Then, even if you do decide to turn it into a larger work in the studio, the feel and atmosphere of a direct painting will already be in the preliminary work.

There are a few tools you can use to help you find an image. Make a viewing frame from black card or some thin plywood. It can be quite small, only a few inches square, but it should be the same shape as your canvas. Look through it and try to isolate the image you want. See the Glossary for details.

Of course, one of the major elements in your composition will be pattern, and while in Project 24 we've looked at pattern on pattern, in Project 25 it's pattern as a picture in itself. This is all about control: control of the brush because it can be quite difficult to keep each stroke even in tone and colour and length, control of the overall pattern so it's as precise at the edges as it is in the middle. Any bright textile with a regular pattern can be used as a model.

Project 26 is extension of subject. New painters often portray their subject with everything in the middle and nothing around it. Here's a multiple choice question where you can isolate any section of this crowded grouping and make a painting.

Finally, a traditional landscape. This is where we need to use many of the skills already touched on in the various projects; composition to find an exciting view, perspective to give it depth and colour to bring it to life.

American Quilt

This is pattern as picture. There's a particular problem to solve – the composition is the same all across the canvas, so the excitement and the impact must come from the quality of controlled brushwork and from the use of colour within such a strict outline.

First practise by making even, careful strokes of the same length and colour. This requires concentration and care – perhaps it will also encourage your appreciation of many modern abstract paintings which use such deliberate and quiet, control. Use a Number 4 flat brush, and hold it nearer the ferrule than usual to help keep your hand steady. A mahl stick might come in handy – it's a long stick, topped with a wrapped clean rag where it rests against the canvas. Hold it in your left hand to provide your right wrist with something to lean against.

Now turn the single strokes into corners, keeping the turn absolutely clean. The use of close but still distinctly different colours is also important; the original quilt created a three-dimensional pattern by using colour and darker and lighter tones, and you are doing the same.

Look carefully at the darker red, for example. It's not made up of red with black, it's red with purple. Mix each colour on your palette, then mix its related colour before you start to paint.

You can repeat the project with any patterned fabric, or a piece of wallpaper, a shawl… anything with related colours and varying tones. It will be surprisingly difficult to achieve the different reds, for example, and that's part of the learning process, so don't choose a pattern with strong contrasts – it's the subtlety of almost-identical colours which will help you when you begin in mixing shadows and folds in other, more traditional paintings.

Kitchen Still Life

One of the underlying difficulties that most new painters have is a tendency to centre an image on the paper and then somehow blank out the rest of the canvas.

While sometimes that can be very effective – for a portrait or a deliberately isolated object – as a general rule it leaves the painting looking unfinished and the viewer vaguely dissatisfied. Life is not so neat, and our eyes usually see quite a long way to the left and right, above and below, even if the focus is directly in front of us.

Making use of that natural width of vision helps to create a more interesting painting, with lots of different things going on. As you become more skilled you can try creating entire little scenes or details which tell their own story around, behind and in the corners of your paintings.

The first problem-solving exercise is to learn to look at the edges. Set up a table as full of bits and pieces as your kitchen equipment will allow. Try to get a balance, so there are lots of different sizes and shapes. Make sure you have at least three or four feet of crowded tabletop.

Sit down and look. Find a brighter colour or a bigger shape that will be the focus, preferably not right in the middle. Try closing your eyes for a minute, then open them very quickly for one brief look and close them again. The image in your mind will usually be one object that stood out for whatever reason, and that's a good place to start.

Sketch in the tabletop using brown or grey. Make sure at this stage that you keep to the overall muddle, putting everything in so that you are almost painting off the side of the canvas!

When you finish painting all the objects, start thinking about how you are going to make that focal object stand out. Sometimes, as happened to me with this sketch, you have to paint everything before it becomes obvious that you need an additional edge to catch the eye. I made a jug yellow instead of white and the whole picture lit up. While it's useful to have real things in front of you for form, dimension and shape, never be afraid to add something that may not be there.

River Valley

To my mind landscapes are one of the most beautiful and satisfying subjects to paint, no matter what the medium. However, I have to admit that oil painting, so generous and adaptable in other ways, does make it more difficult to paint outdoors directly from nature.

There are two approaches to this problem; first, meet it head on, and just take all your equipment with you, including a travelling easel, a big box of paints, a handful of brushes, a folding chair, an umbrella for the rain, and – very important – a good packed lunch.

Or second, acknowledge the difficulties and learn to make sketches in watercolour, pastel or a limited palette of oil colours, jot down copious notes and colour swatches of what you can see, and if possible use a camera and take snapshots to nudge your memory once you get home.

In truth, of course, we all use both approaches depending on the circumstances, the time of year, the weather, the availability of transport and so on.

For this project I worked on an oil sketch made during the summer when I was on holiday in Spain. The important problem here was the very long view which needed perspective to make the river and the hills vanish behind the mountain on my left.

Natural landscapes like this don't benefit particularly from the grid lines and geometric tricks of formal perspective – you can use the colour and image to create all the depth you need, and that's what we call aerial perspective. All it takes is observation.

There are two aspects of perspective here – the shapes grow smaller and less distinct as they recede and all colours become lighter and less distinct, too, turning to a shadowy blue far out on the horizon.

Practise by first making the colour recede in a graduated band, and then seeing how a river or, for that matter, a road or a valley, will grow more narrow and blurry the further away it is.

That is all you are going to use, and it will be quite enough. Remember that the foreground will not only be darker but crisper and more detailed, so that rocks and pebbles will be clearly shown, while as the hill goes back it also becomes just splodges of brown and cream.

PART TEN:
SUMMING UP

These last three projects are a summing up where you can use all the skills and confidence which you have gained by following the different projects in the book. They are not an end, though, just a pause in what I hope will be an enjoyable future.

Although we have set out various examples, you shouldn't feel bounded by their specific subjects or ideas. From these original projects you could develop literally hundreds, even thousands of sketches and paintings.

Never be discouraged by something that doesn't quite work out the first time. Try anything and everything; every single trial is a lesson from which you can take something away with you. You will learn as much from your disasters as from your triumphs.

As I said, painting with oils outdoors is not always convenient, but don't let that stop you from going out to sketch in oils – that's when a light box, a minimum number of paints and an oil sketching pad will come in useful.

But even when you can't get out, don't think a studio painting needs to be stuffy or dull. Learn to look inside your home for patterns and fabrics, for rich colours in fruit, in vegetables, in china and even in gift wrapping paper from Christmas presents.

Painting is a wonderful part of life: it can be a wholly delightful hobby or a serious study. Everyone can come into it through different doors, and every way is worthwhile. I hope I've put you on the doorstep – it's up to you to open the door.

Basket of Hydrangeas

This study is an example of how varied and exciting to the artist even the most obvious subject can be. I began with a very minimal painting – a few twirls of beige for the handle, flecks of a pinky beige for the dried flowers. Then I tried adding a background, and unhappily my minimal painting vanished into less than the minimum.

So I started again, because the more I looked at the basket the more interesting it became. First is the problem of an enclosing shape, which musn't become overwhelming. Then the flowers, all muted beiges in at least twenty tones, yet none of them very strong. And finally, the tiny shapes that had to be pulled together into the heads and bunches of flowers.

This time I began with a beige sketch to establish the shapes and to make sure I filled the canvas from side to side. When you have something at an angle, you can be fooled into thinking it's smaller than it should be.

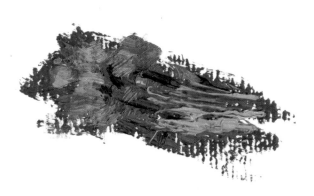

Next came the basket; you should be trying to suggest the twining reeds rather than detail each stalk. Lay a little background first, and then try out how few strokes you need to make it look like a handle. Your sketches may be very different because baskets have varying handles, but they are almost all made up of parallel curving shapes, and you need enough, and closely laid enough, to make a coherent shape.

Try suggesting the bunches of flowers with a dry medium brush, and very lightly touch and drag for a second, touch and drag, broad for the heads and on the edge of the brush for the thin spiky stalks. The clumps of moss should be laid down with the broad edge, too.

Finally, when you begin the project, think back to some of the points we have covered. Make sure the basket fills the whole canvas, choose a background that will be distinct but quietly blend into the overall colouring, and mix your flower colours very carefully so that they are subtly related rather than clashing.

Putting one bunch spilling out over the edge helps to give the basket depth and dimension.

And as a last touch, add a change of colour to the background to make the tablecloth fall away; like the vase in Project 14, it helps to set the basket firmly on a table instead of an anonymous surface.

Garden Fences

This is a subject that many of us see regularly from our windows, but it was the receding fences that made me realize how much aerial perspective could be used to paint this particular view.

The first trial was to make sure I had the recession carefully mapped on the canvas. I wanted the fences to be the stars of the show, so I sketched their top edges in charcoal first, rubbing out a few times until they were just where I wanted them, taking up two thirds of the picture. Landscapes can have a variable amount of sky, and that changes the entire effect. Look back at Project 27 for a much more spacious feeling, full of open air and soft light.

In this case it was the overwhelming pattern of wood slats which was the dominant feature, and so the sky has retreated to just a glimpse of blue up in the corner.

The effect is almost claustrophobic, which is exactly what I wanted. Just a few inches more of sky and the sky would begin to compete with the gardens for our attention.

Try out various slat patterns to give the painting variety. These were quite varied already, but remember, change nature when you want to.

Finally, you can add a few touches: the line of washing, a rambling rose – whatever catches your fancy and would seem appropriate. Hopefully you will begin to appreciate how many paintable views there are even when you don't move from your studio or bedroom window. Upstairs windows are particularly useful because they give us a new perspective on the world. Pissarro's views of Paris, almost all painted from at least four or five stories up, are an example to all of us.

The leaves are just splodges, not so very different from the celery leaves way back in Project 1. Make sure the colour varies, though, because when you look at a landscape like this full of billowing trees and shrubs you'll never be able to count all the greens you can see.

The other aspect of aerial perspective is the change from detail to blur. See how the fences change from quite large, distinct slats to tiny strokes of white right at the back.

A Woman

As a final project, this is our first attempt at a portrait. I've left it until last, because although most painters enjoy trying their hand at portraits, it's also disappointing when it seems impossible to get a likeness of the person sitting so patiently in front of you.

For your first try I suggest you ask someone to sit for you without promising the sitter or yourself that it will be a portrait as such.

Painting the human face, with all its subtle tones and shapes, is the aim here. An individual likeness can come later, as your drawing skills increase and as your observation becomes honed with use.

In any study like this, painting the skin tones will be the greatest single factor in success. I wouldn't recommend buying one of the colours mistakenly named flesh. I find they are all too pinky for anyone except the youngest new-born baby. And strangely enough, you won't start with mixing a pink at all, but with lots of white and only a touch of yellow ochre.

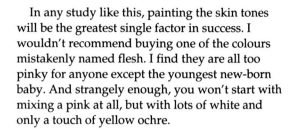

Look carefully at your sitter as you add a little bit of cadmium red. We have such different complexions that there is no formula which will automatically serve everyone, and you'll have to adjust the mixture accordingly.

For Asian or brown skins, begin with white, too, adding just a little burnt umber, and a very light touch of yellow ochre and cadmium red until you get the right mix. Raw umber will be too cold and black for most skins, while burnt umber has just a touch of red in it already to make it warm and life-like. In fact, modelling the shadows with a touch of burnt umber works well with any colour skin.

Once you have the skin tones, the features can be added by marking them in first with white to give you shape, and then with the darker tones to add depth and roundness.

In any portrait the sitter's face should predominate, so let the background fade away. Sweep in the hair as generously as you can with broad strokes rather than details, and the same for the dress. However, don't let the background fade too much around the edges or it will always look unfinished. Covering the surface is important in oil painting, even if it's quiet and neutral in tone.

Shopping guide

Paints

Oil paint has a number of special advantages which have made it the favoured medium since the 16th century, although there had been examples of its use before then. With the switch to canvas instead of board, their easy portability and variable size became an additional advantage. Add the richness of colour and the ease of application when pigment is dissolved in the oil medium, and it's easy to see why oil painting has taken first place in the estimation of the majority of professional and leisure artists.

There are also a few disadvantages with oil: it takes quite a long time to dry, and it can lose that rich intensity as it dries. It will often benefit from varnishing, and with age the varnish may yellow and crack. However, there are new products on the market all the time to help reduce drying time, and to give a more permanent varnish that doesn't fade or yellow.

Try to keep in touch with these at your local shop or by reading some of the very good magazines that are published for artists at all levels of achievement.

Starting to choose your pigments can be bewildering, mainly because of the huge range of colours available. However, in the long term you will find this a real convenience; it is sometimes more difficult to mix colours in oil from the primary red, yellow and blue, so the manufacturers have done the work for you.

Different brands may label the same colour under a proprietary name, but a quick look at an open tube should help you avoid duplication.

Generally there are only two grades of oil paint available: student and artist's quality. The first is cheaper because the pigment has been extended with additives and it will not be as finely ground.

However, some of the basic palette colours are usually perfectly acceptable in student's grade: whites, cadmium yellow, yellow ochre, cadmium red, alizarin crimson, burnt umber, viridian green, ultramarine and ivory black.

But once you have started really enjoying yourself, do add some artist's quality tubes to your box. They are more finely ground, they have few or no additives, and the intensity of colour is incomparable. Some of the subtle colours are not even sold in the cheaper grades.

One of the unique advantages of oil is that you can physically move it about, by scraping off a patch that doesn't work quite as well as you would like, right back to the canvas.

Grinding your own colours is quite easy today and many good household paint shops carry pure pigment at considerable savings. But it's really only worth doing to achieve special effects or if you want an unusual texture. I'd recommend buying a specialist instruction book before you waste time and money.

Acrylic paints often have different names from oil colours, and the range is much more limited. You'll need a special acrylic primer for your canvas, gloss or matt mediums for mixing instead of linseed oil and turpentine, and a different kind of brush cleaner, too.

Although acrylics have the great advantage of drying very quickly, and they are less likely to harden with age or change colour, I must say I prefer traditional oil. But working with one or the other really becomes a matter of personal choice.

Oil colours are already mixed with a small amount of oil to help them flow. The actual amount will vary depending on the weight and absorption of the pigment – earth colours made from natural clays like yellow ochre tend to be heavier than the newer colours mixed in the laboratory.

You can use most oil paints directly from the tube without any additions, or you can add various oils to make them flow more easily and increase their lustre. Turpentine will make them more transparent. The glossary lists the most commonly used oils: linseed, poppy, and walnut. Each has its own properties, but although expensive, linseed oil is probably the best for all-round work.

True turpentine, made from the resin of pine trees, is also expensive, but I never use white spirit (sometimes called turpentine substitute) for mixing oil paints; it is usually full of impurities, and in my experience it can affect the more subtle colours very badly.

However, there are new techniques which produce better quality, and which may make a purer essence.

Most artists begin a new work using 'lean' paint; that is, paint which is either unmixed or with a very small amount of turpentine which allows it to coat the surface. It will be very opaque, and the colours are likely to dry out a little and become fairly flat compared to the squiggles still on your palette. Lean washes provide the best background for any style or subject.

Gradually, the painter will add more turpentine and oil to achieve richer and richer colouring, and greater depth of intensity and tone. This is called 'fat' paint, and so in professional shorthand an artist works from lean to fat.

Highlights are almost always mixed with oil instead of turpentine to add a little gloss and sparkle as the pigment catches the light.

Glazes are made from mixing oil, turpentine, varnish and a tiny bit of colour. The result is a transparent film of colour on top of the original painting. By changing the colour of the glaze, or making it darker or lighter, you can achieve quite remarkable three-dimensional effects similar to a film of coloured cellophane being laid over a light.

To sum up, here is a colour shopping list for the beginner who needs to be equipped from scratch. It's better to buy exactly what you want rather than spend money on a ready-made box which has only some of what you need.

BASIC PALETTE
Flake White
Cadmium Yellow
Yellow Ochre
Cadmium Red
Alizarin Crimson
Burnt Umber
Viridian Green
Ultramarine Blue
Ivory Black
ADD THESE AS YOU PROGRESS
Titanium White
Lemon Yellow
Purple
Indian Red
Light Green
Raw Sienna
Raw Umber
Cerulean Blue
Cobalt Blue
Prussian Blue
Lamp Black

Easels and Extras

For outdoor painting it's useful to have a simple travelling easel with adjustable legs. You can use it at home as well, and avoid buying two.

Once you begin in earnest, a big wooden paint box with fold-down legs is a real boon. It can stand beside you outdoors. Most have a fitted palette which can also be used at home. Second-hand ones often turn up at boot sales and markets.

Brushes

Because oil paintings were meant to be viewed from a reasonable distance, the artist needed brushes that were long enough to let him see the effect of what he was doing.

Old-fashioned brushes were even longer than our present-day versions – Renaissance artists had brushes which they could flourish in a way that only orchestral conductors can now enjoy.

However, the most important aspect for a beginner is comfort. Brushes from different manufacturers and even different ranges by the same maker come in varied lengths, so try them out in the store by moving back and forth in front of an easel until you have found the right length for you.

Brushes come in various sizes from the smallest at Number 0 to the largest, Number 10. They can be made of sable or bristle, the best bristle being hog's hair. All round brushes can be slicked to a fine point. Hog's hair can be round or flat, sloping towards one end or straight across. Avoid cheap synthetic brushes; they are a false economy, difficult to use and liable to come apart or throw hairs constantly.

I use two big, fat house decorator's brushes, 2 inches wide, for blending and for the first wide strokes that establish earth and sky. Since I do a lot of landscape painting, I keep one for blues and one for greens. Even though I am careful about washing them out each time, a flake of the wrong colour can turn up just when you want a pure, clean tone!

When you start painting you'll be able to get by with the few brushes recommended in the introduction to Part One, but soon you'll need to go further. This list may seem to suggest a great many brushes but as soon as you start painting regularly you'll see how useful it is to have one for each colour on your palette. Otherwise you will spend all your time cleaning off the paint before you can use that brush again.

Working with brushes laid down carefully by the side of the easel is possible in oil because the paint dries so slowly. You can also hold three or four brushes in your palette hand, ready every time you want to add just a speck or a highlight.

If you have to stop for a few hours, you can wrap the brushes in cling film and they will stay moist and ready to use.

But when you have finished a session, all the brushes should be completely cleaned off with a little turpentine and then washed carefully in soap and water. Be careful to make sure the handles and the ferrule are clean, too, not just the hair.

Never be afraid to spend money on good brushes – I've had some of mine since I was twelve years old, and they are as soft as they were when I attended art school.

MINIMUM BRUSH SHOPPING LIST
1 small sable round (Number 0)

1 medium hog's hair, flat
(Number 4)

1 medium hog's hair round
(Number 6)

1 large hog's hair flat
(Number 10)

ONCE YOU START TO WORK
3 small hog's hair, round and flat
(Numbers 1, 2, 3)

1 medium sable round
(Number 4)

1 medium sable round
(Number 6)

2 large hog's hair, flat
(Numbers 8 and 9)

If you haven't got a purpose-made box you'll need some sort of protection for your brushes when you go outside to paint. You can make a brush holder out of two pieces of thick card, with the brushes sandwiched between them. Three or four elastic bands at top and bottom will keep them safe. You'll also need a double dipper to clip to your palette and hold small quantities of oil and turpentine while you work, although at home, two small ceramic cups will do nicely.

A few rags will keep your hands clean. A drawer of old bits of cloth will come in handy all year round.

Canvas and Other Supports

There is almost no limit to the kinds of surface on which you can paint in oil. As with no other medium, the entire canvas is usually covered, and the only part obvious to the viewer is the weave, rough or smooth, of the fabric itself. Even that is becoming less common as many modern artists use thick layers of pigment.

Choose your canvas according to the grain of the fabric, called 'tooth'; this applies to all supports:

Use rough surfaces for large pictures where you'll be splashing on the pigment with abandon!

Fine-grained cloth, where the bumps won't send your brush off in the wrong direction, is best for highly detailed painting

A medium grain is useful for everything in between.

For outdoor sketching and all preliminary work, I use specially prepared pads of oiled paper. These come in various finishes, just like canvas, and in typical paper sizes of A4, A3 and so on.

They do have some disadvantages – they can't be re-used, and you have to work carefully if you are scraping away the paint layers to get back to the base. There is also a tendency for the paper to curl up at the edges as it dries, after you have painted on one side. Otherwise, they are a very useful addition to the oil painters' kit, and today I wouldn't be without one or two pads in the car in case I see something really marvellous. In fact, although it's not recommended, I use both sides for sketching, making good use of every square centimetre.

Another modern convenience are canvas boards. These come already prepared, primed and ready to paint, and being on fairly heavy cardboard, they are much lighter to carry and store than traditional canvas on its heavy wooden frames.

Canvas, the best support for your painting, can be bought in rolls or, more expensively, already stretched. Making the stretchers can be a good project for a week's rainy afternoons – if you make three or four in the sizes you prefer, you will be prepared for your next few sessions, and they can be primed and allowed to dry without haste. However, for the beginner, I would suggest buying a few ready-made canvases, either as boards or on stretchers, until you sort out your own personal preferences for size and texture.

You can also use hardboard in panels, plywood or metal. All of these need to be rubbed down before you start, to give the paint something to key into. You may need three or four coats of primer to give you a good working support.

Whatever surface you choose, keep away from synthetic fabrics, unless they have been specially prepared for oil painting. The oil in the pigment can dissolve them, and before I learned about this reaction, I had found little holes in some of my most successful paintings.

Glossary

Aerial perspective:
This is the natural combination of human vision and the Earth's atmosphere. Aerial perspective relies on two major phenomena: that what is in the foreground grows darker, larger and more distinct the nearer it is to the watching eye, and that what is the background grows lighter, smaller, and hazier, the further it is from the eye.

An additional effect is that any background will grow slightly blueish as it recedes.

Alla prima:
Technique in which the final surface of a picture is completed at one sitting, without underpainting. It was typical of the French Impressionists who loved to go out on painting trips, often comparing their completed works at the end of the day.

Binder:
Any substance which holds pigment together and helps it to adhere to a surface. Most commonly oil and wax.

Bloom:
Discoloured film that appears with age on varnished surfaces, causing a slightly white opaque surface. It will disappear when the old varnish is cleaned off.

Bole:
Browny red clay sometimes used as a material for underpainting. It may show through eventually when the pigments on top fade or become abraded through poor storage.

Cadmiums:
Group of pigments made from cadmium sulphates and noted for their brilliance and permanence.

Chiaroscuro:
The effect of light and shade in a painting, derived from the Italian for 'bright-dark'. Usually it refers to paintings with strong tonal contrasts, most especially of scenes at night or with dark backgrounds and with controlled sources of light like a lamp or a fire.

Colour wheel:
Most art students are asked to paint a colour wheel. The centre is made up of equal parts of the three primary colours, red, blue and yellow. These are primary because they cannot be created by mixing.

Around that is a band made up of the colours created by mixing adjoining primaries: green from blue and yellow, orange from red and yellow, purple from red and blue. These are called the secondary colours.

Finally the outer wheel is made up of the tertiary colours, where the secondary colours are mixed back with the primaries creating mixtures of three colours, 'broken' colours rather than pure colours.

Complementary colours:
A colour having the maximum contrast with another colour on the wheel; orange, a mixture of red and yellow, is the complementary of and opposite to blue on the wheel.

Composition:
A much-misused word, which simply describes the arrangement of form, shape and colour in a painting.

If you make a quick sketch or underpainting on the canvas, then obvious faults can be corrected. Later you can start thinking about colour composition, tonal composition, and so on.

But for those who are just beginning, composition should not become a stumbling block. If the painting covers the canvas, and it represents the colours you had in your mind when you started, and it shows the subject in the way that you wanted, then the result should be an accurate representation of what you intended, and that is a successful painting.

As your skill increases everything, including the finer points of composition, will begin to make more sense and provide a firmer base for continuing development.

Extender:
Material added to pigment and oil to increase the bulk.

Ferrule:
The wide metal ring on a brush which connects the handle to the head.

Filbert:
A brush whose bristles form a flat, tapering shape.

Framing:
It's often difficult to separate a good

subject from the panorama in front of you. Make a couple of card viewing frames, one square and one rectangular. Their cut-out centres should be roughly 2" x 2" (5 x 5 cm) and 2" x 3" (5 x 8 cm). Paint both sides black. When you hold one up to an eye, and close the other eye, it will be as if you were looking through the viewfinder of a camera.

Fugitive:
Term applied to some colours which fade especially badly when exposed to light for a long time. Purples, mauves and lilacs are particularly prone to this.

Gesso:
A mixture of gypsum and glue used as a primer on panels and canvas to provide a smooth, brilliant white surface. Miniature painters often use gesso even today in order that every detail can be smoothly painted.

Glaze:
A translucent layer that changes the colour underneath. Painters like Constable used glaze on top of glaze to achieve an effect of distance and glimmering colour.

Hue:
The title of a colour, that which distinguishes blue, say, from yellow.

Impasto:
Paint applied very thickly to create a textured surface.

Key:
The prevailing tone in a painting. A predominantly light painting is said to

have a high key, a predominantly dark one a low key.

Lightfast, Permanent:
Colours which do not easily fade in light. In truth, all paint fades eventually so 'permanent' is not truly accurate, but permanent or lightfast colours do last much longer than fugitive ones. Tubes of paint are labelled appropriately.

Local colour:
The actual colour of an object (insofar as the human eye can see it) unmodified by distance or reflection. Far-away mountains will have a local colour of green even though they look blue.

Mastic:
Resin obtained from trees and used to make varnish.

Mixing Oils:
Oil paints are mixed with various oils to aid the flow of the paint, to dilute them and to add gloss to the finished brushstroke. These are the most common:

LINSEED OIL
Made from flax, linseed is used both raw and boiled. The best general product for artists is cold-pressed or cold test oil. It is pale yellow in colour, it dries in three or four days, and its only fault is a tendency to yellow with age, which is why it is sometimes avoided where brilliant white or pastel colours are required.

POPPY OIL
This is paler than linseed, and it takes longer to dry: up to seven days, even in a thin layer of paint. However, it seems less liable to yellow with age, and is used more with whites and pale colours.

WALNUT OIL
Traditionally used for pale colours, this is now more or less superseded by poppy oil, because of its tendency to go rancid if not stored carefully.

Tint:
The lightening of a colour. When you add white to an original pigment to make a lighter tone, it is a tint of the original.

Tone:
Describes the degree of darkness or lightness of a colour.

Varnishes:
COPAL VARNISH
Made from a resin which has orange in the final product, it tends to create a warm glow over the painting. When this is suitable for the subject, then copal is ideal, but be warned: it is very likely to darken even more with age.

DAMAR RESIN
The most commonly used and popular varnish; it is a natural product, and ages well with little yellowing. It can also be dissolved in turpentine to make a removable varnish. Damar is less likely to crack or to bloom than other varnishes.

Vanishing Point:
In perspective, a point on the horizon where receding parallel lines appear to meet.

Index

Many of these terms appear throughout the book, but the page numbers refer to the most important and specific references. The painting project titles are in italics.